357052

Life PROJECTS k

D0514163

Vicki Yates

Heinemann
LIBRARY

H www.heinemann.co.uk/library
Visit our website to find out more information about Heinemann Library books.

To order:
☎ Phone 44 (0) 1865 888066
🖹 Send a fax to 44 (0) 1865 314091
🖳 Visit the Heinemann Bookshop at www.heinemann.co.uk/library to browse our catalogue and order online.

First published in Great Britain by Heinemann Library, Halley Court, Jordan Hill, Oxford OX2 8EJ, part of Pearson Education. Heinemann is a registered trademark of Pearson Education Ltd.

© Pearson Education Ltd 2008
First published in paperback in 2009
The moral right of the proprietor has been asserted.

Editorial: Charlotte Guillain and Vicki Yates
Design: Victoria Bevan, Joanna Hinton-Malivoire and Q2A solutions
Picture research: Ruth Blair and Q2A solutions
Production: Duncan Gilbert

Printed and bound in China by South China Printing Co. Ltd.

ISBN 978 0 431 191874 (Hardback)

ISBN 978 0431 19195 9 (Paperback)
13 12 11 10 09
10 9 8 7 6 5 4 3 2 1

British Library Cataloguing in Publication Data
Yates, Vicki. Life at work. - (Then and now)
1. Work - Social aspects - Juvenile literature 2. Work environment - Juvenile literature 3. Work - Social aspects - History - Juvenile literature 4. Work environment - History - Juvenile literature I. Title
306.3'6
A full catalogue record for this book is available from the British Library.

Acknowledgements
The publishers would like to thank the following for permission to reproduce photographs:
Bionikmedia p. **22**; Collections of The Historical Society of Princeton p. **18**; Corbis pp. **10** (Baldwin H. Ward & Kathryn C. Ward), **12** (EFE), **13** (Left Lane Productions) **15** (Jonny Le Fortune/Zefa); Enco p. **11** (Jan Napieralski, Poland); Ford Media p. **21**; GM Motors p. **20**; Getty Images p. **5**; John Deere p. **9**; Library of Congress p. **14**; New York Picture Library p. **6**; Photolibrary.com pp. **16**, **17** (Index Stock Imagery), **19** (Photo Researchers, Inc); Science & Society Picture Library p. **4** (Colin T Gifford); Shutterstock p. **23**; Staffordshire County Records Office pp. **8**, **23**; Valtra Media p. **7**, **23**.

Cover photographs reproduced with permission of Corbis: farmer (Bettmann), tractor (Lester Lefkowitz). Back cover photograph of car factory reproduced with permission of GM Motors.

Every effort has been made to contact copyright holders of any material reproduced in this book. Any omissions will be rectified in subsequent printings if notice is given to the publishers.

Contents

What is work?

Work is the jobs people do. People have jobs to earn money.

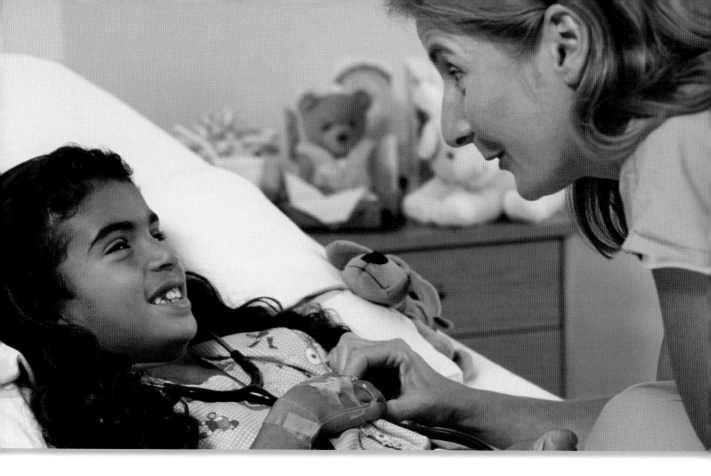

Work has changed over the years.

Different jobs

plough

Long ago farmers used a horse and plough.

Today farmers can use a tractor and plough.

Long ago builders used small tools.

Today builders can use machines.

Long ago people sewed clothes by hand.

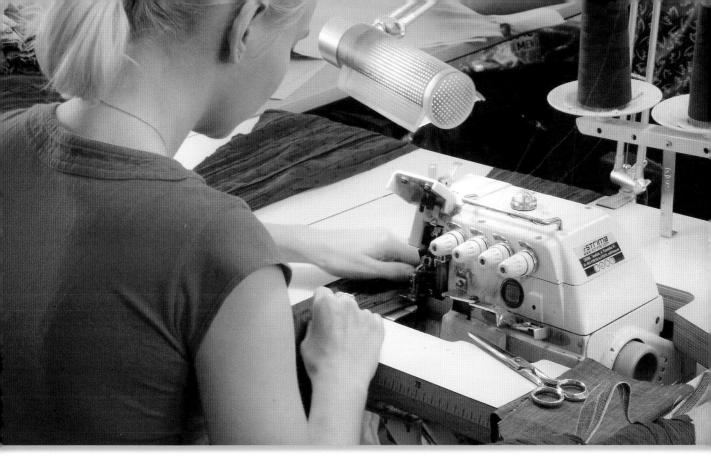

Today people can make clothes with machines.

Long ago people in shops counted money in their heads.

Today people in shops count money
with a till.

Long ago people wrote with typewriters.

Today people write with computers.

Long ago doctors visited sick people
at home.

Today we go to see a doctor in a surgery when we are ill.

Long ago delivery drivers used horses and carts.

Today delivery drivers use lorries.

Let's compare

Long ago work was very different.

Which is better? Then or now?

Who are they?

What job do these men do? Think how it is different now.

Answer on p. 24

Picture glossary

 **money** people use money to buy things

 **plough** something farmers use to turn soil over

 **tool** something that helps you do a job

Index

Answer to question on p. 22: They are firemen.

Note to Parents and Teachers

Before reading
Ask the children what jobs they would like to do when they are older. What jobs do their parents do? What time do their parents go to work? Explain that long ago people had to work very hard and for very long hours. Even children had to work in factories and mines.

After reading
• Talk about how each shop sold a special thing, for example, greengrocers sold vegetables and fruit. There would be a separate bread shop and a separate fish shop. Make two different shops in the class room. You will need fruit and vegetables for a greengrocers and a mix of produce for the supermarket. Invite the children to lay out the vegetables and fruit and label and price the produce for the greengrocers. Put the supermarket goods onto shelves and pack the fruit and vegetables in cling film. Invite some children to be either greengrocers or on a till. Ask other children to go shopping. What differences do they notice?
• Tell the children the nursery rhyme: "Naughty Pauty, Jack-a-Dandy/Stole a piece of sugar candy/From the grocer's shoppy shop/And away did Hoppy hop." Ask the children how they know this is an old rhyme.